The South Hams
in Colour

Chips Barber

Boat Trip on the Dart

Welcome aboard for a voyage through the beautiful South Hams, quite probably the most lovely part of Devon. Here we start with a familiar sight at Dartmouth. It's a fine day for a river cruise so the various vessels that ply the Dart up to Totnes do very well on days like this.

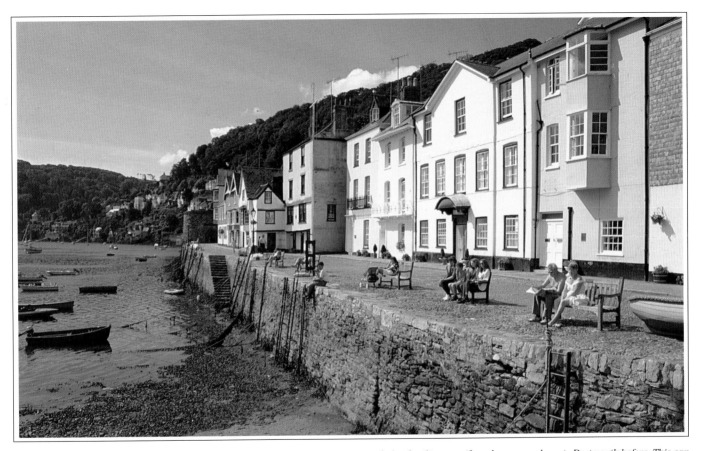

Dartmouth

This is Bayards Cove at Dartmouth, a place that you may feel is familiar even if you have never been to Dartmouth before. This can be easily explained for this fine line of old waterfront buildings has 'starred' in many television programmes, commercials and films. It shared the part of Liverpool in 'The Onedin Line' with Exeter. Incidentally, when 'The French Lieutenant's Woman' was made, Exeter was played by Kingswear as Exeter had changed too much since Victorian times. Bayards Cove has a timeless feel about it so it has also been thoroughly convincing as 'Aberdeen', a German fishing port and a host of other places. Many famous actors have walked its cobble stones and have enjoyed the ever-changing river scene, a hive of activity, particularly during the summer months.

Dartmouth
Dartmouth is very much a maritime town with the waterfront dominating the scene. This picture shows the small harbour known as The Boat Float, which lives up to its name when the tide is in. Surrounding it are buildings that are all different in size and shape and if you glance upwards, when you next walk around the town, you will see a wonderful variety of architecture but make sure that the many seagulls, who are a vociferous bunch, do not shower you in an abundance of 'good luck', bestowed in their own inimitable style.

Dartmouth

If you are the observant type you will notice that there is a lot of bunting about in this colourful picture. This was taken at regatta time, a sequence of days when the town is at its busiest with a tide of visitors pouring in. Most of them are very sensible types who wisely like to walk around the town centre or promenade along the two embankments, North and South, all of which is fairly easy on the feet as this part of the town is unusually flat. However, away from this reclaimed flat land, once part of the estuary, Dartmouth is a town of mountainous hills. The back streets of the old part of the town have numerous flights of steps – wonderful if you are a fitness fanatic with energy to burn, not so good if you are not! The hill in the background is where the pictures on the next two pages were taken so perhaps we have saved you a climb up Devonshire's Alps!

Dartmouth and Kingswear

But what a view! This pair of pictures show that sometimes the effort expounded is worth it for the reward is a glimpse of 'Heaven'. This is the Dart in all its glory. Seen from this aerie the Lower Ferry, referred to as a floating bridge, can be spied on its way across the Dart from Kingswear, a journey it does with great regularity.

The mouth of the River Dart
The river starts as a number of trickles on the high moors of Dartmoor. The East and West Dart Rivers combine flows at the famous beauty spot of Dartmeet to flow through a deep and wooded gorge to leave the moors and flow on, over a series of rapids, down to Totnes. This is the tidal limit and soon the river broadens out into a deep, wide and twisting estuary, christened by no lesser personage than Queen Victoria as 'The English Rhine'. In the distance, on the hillside, is a tower standing on the hill, a landmark, known as the Daymark, which can be seen for many miles. It was built in 1864 by the Dart Harbour Commissioners. In the past this was an important daytime-only navigation aid to shipping as the mouth of the Dart was not that easily spotted from the sea. This landmark is accessible by foot with a car park close by for those who do not want to walk too far to see the impressive, hollow, Grade II listed building.

Dartmouth Castle

These two pictures are taken at Dartmouth Castle, a popular spot with both visitors and locals alike for it's the perfect place from which to set off for a coastal walk, with some wonderful scenery along the cliffs to Little Dartmouth and beyond towards Stoke Fleming. (Left) In this view Kingswear Castle, on the opposite bank of the river, can be seen. Behind and above it the coastal footpath to Berry Head and Brixham is well hidden in the vegetation. It's a remarkable walk but one that should only be undertaken by the fittest of individuals for the cliff path rises and falls with alarming regularity so what might appear to be a comfortable walk on the map can turn out to be a tough ramble. Nevertheless it's a wonderful section of coastline and one that should not be missed. The castles guard the entrance to the Dart, well located to help repel invading forces, for down the centuries Dartmouth was singled out for attacks on a number of occasions. To further help in the defence of the port a large chain was strung across the river from Dartmouth Castle to a point not far from Kingswear Castle on the far bank. This was given the nickname of "Old Jawbones". Dartmouth Castle is open to the public and well worth a visit for it is steeped in history. It's a pity the stout stone walls cannot speak! The church at Dartmouth Castle is dedicated to St Petrox and must have one of the best views in the county.

Blackpool Sands

Blackpool Sands couldn't be more different to the matching place name in Lancashire and you will have to make your own mind up which is the more beautiful as beauty is in the eye of the beholder! This beach, between the villages of Stoke Fleming and Strete, has also been used as a location for many films throughout the years.

Slapton Sands

There is a good reason why these twin flags flutter in the breeze by the beach at Slapton sands. In early 1944 the Americans took over this length of coastline, and some 3,000 acres of the surrounding countryside, to prepare for the D-Day landings in France. The local populace from six villages, and a great number of farms, had to be swiftly evacuated to accommodate the Americans. Sadly, many troops were killed here during the exercises, particularly when the enemy caught them by surprise. In 1994, fifty years after this dramatic episode in South Hams' history, there was another invasion of Americans, many returning to make a nostalgic pilgrimage.

Torcross – the Sherman Tank

If you were looking for a single caption for these two pictures "War and Peace" might be one suggestion. This Sherman tank, probably the most photographed object in the area, was raised from the bed of Start Bay, on 19 May 1984, to be placed in the car park at Torcross, at the southern end of Slapton Ley. It is another poignant reminder of those events in 1944. It has inspired many to go and find out for themselves about the subsequent events of the mass evacuation of the area and the ensuing American occupation. Many, like Leslie Thomas in his 'Magic Army', have been moved to write about these happenings.

Slapton Ley *This is a tranquil scene at Torcross where there are a number of unusual road signs to warn passing motorists that there may be some waddling wayfarers straying onto the highway. But these fine creatures have more sense and are enjoying a relaxing morning at the southern end of Slapton Ley, Devon's largest, natural stretch of freshwater.*

Torcross

Torcross faces eastwards towards a long corridor of open sea so that on those rare occasions when there is an easterly gale, the village faces the full fury of the sea. This community, on the shores of Start Bay, has been battered by storm waves with much damage to property, the storms of January 1979 being one recalled by locals as an awesome spectacle. A new sea wall, engineered to reduce the incredible power of these waves, helps Torcross villagers sleep that bit better when the elements give vent to their fury. This view looks northward along Slapton's golden sands, formed of shingle from a number of sources. Slapton Ley can be seen to the left of the shoreline properties.

Beesands

Beesands is the next village along the coastline towards Start Point and the coastal footpath provides a much more direct line to it from Torcross than the winding road, which goes inland and back out to reach the sea again. Beesands has a special atmosphere of its own with the Cricket Inn almost the jewel in the crown of this small fishing community, a real pub with a friendly welcome for all! The village has not been without its problems and there is sufficient evidence on the walls of the pub to show that this has been a wild place to live when the cruel sea has battered away at the waterfront properties. This picture was taken a short time before a new sea wall, and protective barrier, was constructed to protect the village but at the next village, again just a little way down the coast, it was a very different story...

Hallsands – the ruined village

This is the ruined village of Hallsands, another village where the locals derived their livelihoods from the sea. In the 1890s a license was granted to Sir John Jackson to dredge shingle from the sea at Hallsands. This was to be used in the construction of new docks at Plymouth. Consequently the beach at Hallsands started to disappear, dropping many feet. Every time there was a storm from the general direction of the east, damage to this small village was caused, there being nothing to absorb the immense power of the waves as the beach had done for centuries. On a winter's night in 1917 the village was virtually destroyed and over the years the ruins themselves have been gradually eroded. More details of this and other places along Start Bay can be discovered in my book "From the Dart to the Start". (Opposite) Salcombe is the most southerly town in Devon, a place famed for its mild winters. This aerial picture shows its location on the west side of the estuary, on the left side of the picture, sheltered from the prevailing westerlies. Kingsbridge is at the top left of the picture whilst East Portlemouth is at the bottom centre.

Salcombe

This is how Salcombe looks from the heights of East Portlemouth. In Victorian times, when the railways spread to virtually every town and village in the land, there was talk of a line to Salcombe but the townsfolk had other ideas and a vote was taken not to have one. The nearest station was Kingsbridge, the journey for visitors being completed either by water down the beautiful estuary or by a bumpy old stage coach, which was known to rattle the bones of the most seasoned traveller.

Salcombe *Salcombe is a yachtsman's paradise – the sight of the various sailing craft creates a colourful view. For 'landlubbers' there are golden beaches on both sides of the estuary, the sheltered nature of it making them real sun traps, for those who like that sort of thing!*

Salcombe

This is the colourful South Sands Ferry, which plies up and down the estuary between Salcombe town and, as the name of the ferry implies, South Sands just under a mile away to the south west and closer to the estuary mouth. Many people who come to Salcombe like to sit on one of the many benches that look out over the waterfront, which is a picturesque scene with many comings and goings. It is a therapeutic, passive activity that can condition people to the more relaxed pace of life, enjoyed by many, that attracts people to the South Hams. They say it is also conducive to long life, perhaps the reason why so many people choose to retire here?

Kingsbridge

Kingsbridge sits at the top of the estuary. It's a small bustling town with most of its main street a steep hill – wonderful, calorie-burning exercise for those who toil up it on a regular basis. The focal point is the waterfront, an attractive setting for the town, a sheet of water when the tide is in, a sea of glorious mud when it's out. Some of the more important roads of the South Hams converge on Kingsbridge so it has developed as an important shopping centre.

Bolt Tail *All the pictures in this little book are taken on fine days and none were better than this one, which is taken from the top of a low cliff called the Shippen, at Hope Cove. But bad weather is never that far away and storm-force southwesterlies have doomed several vessels, washed onto the cliffs along this Bigbury Bay coastline. In the top right of this picture is the well-known headland of Bolt Tail where, in 1760, HMS Ramillies came to grief with the loss of over 700 lives. On days like this one it's hard to imagine what tragedies such headlands can cause.*

Hope Cove

This picture is taken from the same spot but with a change of direction. Here we are looking down on Hope Cove, another South Hams settlement where fishing was the principle industry in the past. Today tourism also adds much to the economy of the place for people love to wend their way down the narrow lanes to enjoy Hope Cove's beaches. Those who love walking the coastline often start the spectacular walk to Salcombe from here, a stroll that scales great heights between Bolt Tail and Bolt Head.

Thurlestone

Those who head in the opposite direction will also have a lovely walk, Thurlestone being the next village to be encountered. This settlement takes its name from a rugged old rock, which forms an impressive, resistant arch but, alas, is not seen in this picture even though it is just yards away. This view is of just part of Thurlestone Sands and the small lagoon formed by the beach blocking the access of the stream that reaches the sea here. It's a truly beautiful place but, then again, they all are!

Bantham

This scene is a favourite of photographers and calendar manufacturers. It's taken at the mouth of the River Avon, known by many locals as the Aune, at Bantham. Just around the corner is Bantham's sandy beach, Burgh Island and the open sea of Bigbury Bay. The Avon or Aune's estuary is another sheltered estuary. For part of its way a tidal road runs up its western bank to Aveton Gifford. The pronunciation of this place name has divided communities so it's probably wiser read than said!

Burgh Island and Bigbury on Sea
Burgh Island is what you might call a part-time island. When the tide is in there can be no doubt about its status, but when the tide is out, like it is in this picture, it is linked to the mainland by a sandy causeway. It's widely believed that Agatha Christie wrote two of her novels on the island but if you want to know more you should read "Burgh Island and Bigbury Bay" which covers this immediate area in greater detail.

Burgh Island *What would you call this strange contraption, which ferries people across to the island when the tide is in? 'Sea tractor' is one suggestion for a machine that has evolved over the years to combat the shifting sands and the wind and waves. There have been some 'exciting' journeys across when the windy southwesterlies have contrived to whip up a frenzied sea. Here, though, all is bliss in Bigbury Bay. Even the ghost of Tom Crocker isn't about, haunting the island's historic pub, The Pilchard Inn, where an episode of the BBC's "Lovejoy" was once filmed.*

The Erme Estuary and Mothecombe

The picture above is really what the South Hams is all about. The Erme's estuary is particularly beautiful because it has remained in private hands for more than one and a half centuries, but there are many other inlets that you can freely explore in order to get away from the madding crowd, should you so desire. (Opposite) Mothecombe's beach, at the mouth of the Erme, is a private one, but open to the public on Wednesdays, Saturdays and Sundays. When the tide is out there is an extensive bar of hard sand at the river mouth where the opening and closing sequences of "International Velvet", starring a young Tatum O'Neal riding her horse, were filmed.

Frogmore Creek

This is just such a tidal inlet, Frogmore Creek, one of the many to be a branch of the Kingsbridge Estuary. The creeks look like broad rivers when the tide is in but flatter to deceive as when the tide recedes an expanse of oozing mud is left exposed. All these creeks follow the same pattern as they suddenly end, almost without warning, with a tiny, usually fairly insignificant, stream entering them. Most have a small village at the top of them, these creeks forcing roads to go around them to get anywhere. Frogmore is just out of sight to the right of this view. A public right of way follows the far bank for quite some way, a quiet rural corridor to appreciate the delights of creeks like this.

Ugborough and distant Dartmoor

Had you climbed any of the many hills of the South Hams and looked northwards, you would have glimpsed the sight of Dartmoor, but as there is a sister to this book called "Beautiful Dartmoor" it's had to take a back seat this time. This view is a good example of the South Hams' hilltop view. It shows the village of Ugborough with the rolling moors looming up above in the background. The picture has a certain resemblance to a view of Widecombe with its tall church, but I can assure you that it isn't!

Totnes We finish almost where we came in with a view of the River Dart. This time we are at Totnes, one of the four ancient boroughs of Devon, a wonderful old town full of old buildings, ghosts and a wealth of history that demands more attention. This is particularly true on summer Tuesdays when many folk don Elizabethan clothes to give a real atmosphere to the place. It has been described as "The Gateway to the South Hams" but, sadly from the point of this book, it's the exit. I hope you have enjoyed the few snippets of information and my personal selection of favourite photographs.